Letters To Dead Children

And Other Poems

By

HARRIS STEVENS

Little Daisy Press

Harris Stevens' poetry is holographic. You can't hold it in your hand, but you can feel it in the heart. It is sophisticated, deeply sensitive, sometimes scholarly, often raw, vivid, vulnerable, and honest. Don't be surprised if you find yourself transported to new, multi-faceted depths of awareness.

Charmian Anderson PhD. Author of "The Heart of Success"

PREFACE

This small book of poems was written over many decades. Most of the themes are linked through connections between childhood, death, and the way in which photography and the collection of curious objects establish and strengthen our attachments to the past.

The earlier poems reflect experiments in form and style, and more recently, the topic of transgender issues, specifically what is now referred to as indirect dysphoria. Many of these poems wrote themselves. I put pen to paper, sometimes with only bare-bone ideas in mind.

In part, this book stands as a memorial to the transitory nature of childhood and life itself. It is a collection of poetry ("my children") lovingly gathered, preserved, and hopefully cherished by some future sets of eyes whom by chance may gaze upon them.

Finally, a tip of the hat to *Lewis Carroll, Ludwig Wittgenstein*, and many others who inspired and taught me that a word's meaning is determined by the nature of its context, and that words can be born, and can exist outside of the dictionary if they fulfill a necessary requisite.

To:

Sophie - The Girl in the Mirror

CONTENTS

Girls, Ghosts and Ghastly Things

Harris Stevens

Letters to Dead Children

(Reflections viewing an 1850s Daguerreotype "Girl with Cat")

I.

Dear Adelaide,
I look into dim-gray eyes
that have not seen for a hundred years
Staid budding Youth slouched
in languid repose-never sensing
the confinement of tinted glass.
Baring your naked, off-shouldered Grace
Endowed through an ancient mother's
Prerogative-
Viewed: from far centuries eroticism
Browned by the Sun, though
bathed not in healthful warmth-
Feeling only its timely threat
to dissolve what is left of you.
My imaginings seek to coax you out evoking
brightness once beheld,
What thoughts are these, that lurk
beyond your ridged stare?
And...
What words from frozen, dumb lips
speak so mutely?

You do not fidget as children must
nor sleep- one pictures you
presiding over perpetual garden parties
- the quiet cat, with its smug Victorianism
nestled in your lap
Child!
Empowered to command attentions
of a distant admirer into some fanciful
and equilibrious union,
I shrink from your Ghostly penetration
that dares turn tables and violate me
with vacant Immortality!
Yet....
Eye to eye we rendezvous,
entwined in heart by silver thread.
If memories fix your gazing touch,
Or uproot thee from your earthen bed...

II.

Dear Aida,
Were I to stir your gentle sleep
and still the pale of Death,
Could caresses lift that tender weight?
and gain release, Thus so,
Protect-
Your fragility, I do bequeath, My Liege,
Unto o' slumberous Rest!

The Evil Twin

My dear daughter was never punished
For any digression or little sin
Because she claimed, "I never did so,
It but was my evil twin!"

Tho I searched and searched both high and low
I could not find a trace.
Darling daughter would you fib so boldly to your
father's face?
"No father dear, I would not lie"...
With her head bowed in disgrace
Still, no visage did I spy,
No phantom could I chase
Until my gaze sensed something near,
illusionary based.
With a shushing finger to her lips,
My daughter whispered in my ear,
"Don't make a sound or move around
For my evil twin is here!"
Sure enough, there it was, appearing out of
the blue,
And when I turned towards my darling dear
There be not one, but two!

Harris Stevens

"Oh father dear make it go away,
I promise to be good".
But so did the "other" make its plea
Convincingly from where it stood.
I scratched my head and pondered
This dilemma, and then again,
On and on I pondered still
Which one be the evil twin?
Then one child ran to embrace me,
With reddened face and tear filled eyes
While the other remained quite stoic, soulless in
her disguise.
"Away, away with you!"
I screamed determined
Such a fatherly edict it could not ignore,
And now there was but the two of us,
The evil twin no more.

So if your child comes to you, the devil's deed denied,
Look carefully about her room where an evil twin
may hide!

There be Monsters!

Under the bed or in her head
The monsters are awaiting.
Or may they be, Ah, so might she
The monster of her making?
She lays supine spouting words of rhyme
With a smile so deceiving...
So small and frail, a little girl?
Or the monster of her making?
A beckoning call and that is all,
Concealed by sweet perfume.
But throughout the night you sense something's
not right as you tiptoe into her room.
Awakened from dreams, she turns towards your
screams
The dark portends shadows of Doom
Standing by the door, in fear you deplore...
Stepping stealthy into the gloom.
Then she calls,"Come to me!"..and to obey you
must heed
Approaching while quietly shaking,
A child so frail, just a little girl?
Or the monster of her own making?
With arms outstretched she pulls you to breast

No pulse, nor heartbeat beneath
You embrace for a while
As her mouth quivers, then smiles
Bearing a set of little sharp teeth.
From the tomb be taken
Snatched from the grave for a fee,
A vixen Vernal, Your child Eternal,
Waiting for All Hallow's Eve.
As you hold her, you must!
Only the magik you trust...
Nary a thought of what you've forsaken
What once was, now is, as the spell craft gives...a
Monster of your own making.

If a moral there be.. One might decree
As you kneel before her and pray,
"All little girls are monsters you see...
But in the most wondrous way!"

Jennett, Dorcas, and Rue

Witchy witchy, witchy woo.
Poppets three, Jennet, Dorcas, and Rue.
Their names pay homage to the sisters who
were tortured, imprisoned and abused,
finally hung, then burnt to ash in March, sixteen
hundred and two.
Of spell-craft and witchery they were made to
confess, and they accused their own families too.
And so went the lot to gallows man including little
Jennett, Dorcas and Rue.
In their tattered homespun be-spelled,
with some old and potent voodoo,
The poppets were made by a Cajun-land crone
that had nothing better to do.
She could conjure up devils, or demons galore,
and sometimes Jesus too,
And I wonder which spirit possesses the poppets
Little Jennet, Dorcas and Rue?

Harris Stevens

Little No Name With Shades

She stood in Black!
Little No Name with shades.
The hum-buzzing of the street surrounds her.
Oblivious passers-by and the traffic glide around
Little No Name's frozen form.
But MY eyes, unfazed by HER electra-mag NET
That tugged at the ferro-city of my vignette gaze.
SHE was there!
In Sunshine hair, arms folded, one leg askance
The bulk of her three score pounds supported
By a fatherly sign post.
A decade of breaths....
One hundred and fifty million and counting!
Were her electric blue eyes behind the sun glass,
staring back at me
Confident that she could easily fend off the weight of
the phantasmic?
And..... I, a camera man without his tool
Rolling by at thirty per.....
Capturing the still-life moment on one solitary
brain cell
A doki doki Decora gal
Not yet the mother-goddess of the bus-ways.

Doki Doki- Japanese onomatopoeia "Beating heart"
Decora Gal -a Japanese fashion popular in the mid-2000s

In Memoriam

Her DNA was found among the blood sheets.
Child scent still lingered, thick as maple syrup
in the void of her presence.
The kid-bed laid bare of warmth, pink flannel,
and a love-crushed teddy.
The night's sweet dreams made weak
by the pervasive, unfamiliar cheap cologne
masking sweaty armpits of the forensics.
Her life-givers were THERE!
A scream stuck to their throats,
as fear clawed its way into the imagined
schism like an ultra-hypoglycemic nightmare.
Raven eyes and flouncy hair had vanished
with the odious stranger into the dark
To the nowhere....
Yet: she was there...still.

Her smiles looking out from darkened corners of
the room,
a casual glance in the hallways, and piano top...
Framed in the digital.
Unheeded; the forlorn whispers of the
interlopers..
"No trace, no trace"

Across the avenues,
Another blithely being.
A typical Saturday morning-glory girl
Whose culinary project has transformed the kitchen
(by her unskilled handiwork)
into cupcake hell.
Ten thousand miles, and an ocean away
Familial sake cups tinkle with the obligatory
"mirai e"
And in the West, a Frenchman breaks bread with his
children.....
...and She: whose cries over the little burnt
offerings...
were buried deep, into the dolly face propped up on
the oil-clothed dinette.
Yet....Unaware!
that her budding breast signified the amplitude
of time.
Unaware.....
Of the other stranger, ever present,
who lurked patiently from some silent, shadowy abyss
that only pastoral sleepwalkers know....
Betrayal.....
As if she too had been ripped from the bed of her
childhood,

In the din and clatter of her life
she doesn't heed the whispering of the romantic.
"No more, no more"
In the city there begins a double death
One quick; One quiet.

1) mirai e – Japanese saying, "to the future

"Our Darling"

She laid, "Our Darling"
In gentle repose
The pallor of death offset
By the starched white linen
And tufted brocade
Black crepe and the scent of Roses
Drape thick perfume-
Gathered silk surrounds purity incorporeal
Enshrining angel-flesh torn from the quick
Nestled in deep mahogany, carefully rubbed
To embrace and protect the fallen lamb.
Auburn braids so carefully kept
With China-pink Damask.
Closed eyes, slightly parted
That soft, sallow skin, soon brittle bone....
A dusty cure for the sleeping beauty
Whose haunting, our memories resist.
Such young years stilled...
Among the cacophony of untimely ends
By sickly cough, or trampled beneath a speeding,
wayward omnibus.
Never to taste the mature brazen air
Nor to bear fruit.

Her Godly manner remembered
By shed tears, and reverent silence.
Eternity forestalled
Until the turn of screws, and the shroud
Cover forever, our darling's final gaze into the
Hereafter.

Memento Mori

I gather up the dead, the discarded lives once
cherished.
Now retrieved from dusty bins, antiqued stalls,
And the hodgepodge wares of itinerant flea
marketeers..
I have become curator, a savior, an urban-
collector god
Whose compulsory nature bears witness to the
forgotten...
Gently cared for, assembled proudly on crowded
shelves, possessed, then to be passed on in endless
revolution
Wherein, such Proustian ethic endures...
Artifacts passionately lean against one another
United in mutual protection
Like sleeping sisters lovingly entwined
in the warmth of a shared bed.
Lives once full-bodied, now tangentially live on
vicariously
In old photo albums, personal histories and
bygone mementos

Once savored pleasures tossed away like rotten
apple cores.
On dull, rainy days I appease the gloom by loving
touch,
Here and there, those poor resurrected waifs...
A thick picture-tome from last century's turn
contains faded faces
Barely hanging on by black paper hinges
Which have been affixed to the browned surface.
Unknown personages peer from door stoops,
Behind baby carriages, and street scenes
Smiles competing with the disarray of telephone
poles
Crisscrossed wires like man made spider webs
trailing off in the distance
And the occasional parked Ford, or Packard
town car.
But among the scores of ordinary snaps are two
curious photographs.
With captions burnt into the emulsion.
A man and woman stand proud against the stone
and fern
While white lettering proclaims *"Mr. and Mrs.
Jack London at Wolf-House"*

I sit, pondering the images...
Is this family related to THE Jack London,
dog stories and writer of...?
Or are they the mementos of a glorious day excursion
into the far reaches of virgin Sonoma forests?
A padded pink and blue baby album was lying
next to "old Jack" and his stone house.
It came from faraway Japan to finally rest in the
bottom of a dumpster outside a Sunday estate sale
in Larkspur, California.
The color and black and white neatly arranged
between thick Mylar pages are of a Japanese
family
looking out from the comfort of the *nineteen
sixties*.

Little girls with black fringe, and flowered
kimono,
Stern-faced boys in dark school uniforms stand next
to their Westernized parents in business suits and
sensible shoes,
expressing their brave, fading culture at *Matsuri*.
Tatami mats and the whole 3B class forming a
human
kanji for "peace" in the cut grass.

As the weather lightens, rain ceases to fall
and a feeble ray of sunlight pushes its way
tentatively through the clouds
I pick up an ancient paperweight dome of
polished glass
Containing the avoirdupois of human sadness.
A child, not yet school aged with golden hair
Feigns rest with eyes closed in everlasting sleep.
She, forever in faded burnt sienna caresses
A small lock of hair, aptly bound with purple ribbon
Affixed to its owner's visage, sealed forever in that
silicate tomb
Much as her bones rest eternal in some faraway
crypt.

Mourning Locket

I commune with the dead, the dark veil between
Born from a child's womb -And Dread
The gentle flush portrayed
Loveliness given way to emptiness
Day beyond day.
She rests, dreamless upon her final bed
Tender in musty silken embroidery
Covering the charade.
Within a Locket shaped of gold, rolled in filigree
Cradled by hollow palm though few ounces scant
Woe-some container of over-bearing weight
The dividing scent fills ancient silvered glass.
A child's breath so sweetly drawn still stirs the air
By the deft hand of an artist's craft create
Given life to tinted eye and coral lips
Whose countenance and frozen hair affix to linger
beyond the pale
Both mourners past and mourners be resigned
To suffer your ubiquitous fate.

The Tragic Story of Mary Bell

(Mary Bell-the youngest serial killer on record,
killed at least two children at age 10)

Mary Bell, the girl from Hell
Did her deed in a concrete dell
Her little friend Norma was there as well.
Two souls lost to urban blight
No one to heed their desperate plight.
Take scissors, a razor, "Lets have some fun"
All to be blamed on the "other one"
"We Murder!!" By childish hands the note said
And when it was over, two lads lay dead.
One with letters carved into his skin
Just so you knew where "THEY" had been.
No compassion given, no compassion felt
As Newcastle suffered what Mary had dealt
They damaged her body, they damaged her mind
Was it surprising she responded in kind?
First trial, then prison, locked up in a cell
Went poor little Mary, the child from Hell.
They opened the gate, they opened the door
Twelve long years later, a wee lass no more
Some memories fade, and some have remained
But England still shudders when they mention her
name.

First Martin, then Brian, had it all been a game?
The township is quiet, but doors are now locked,
The playgrounds are empty where children once
flocked.
Echo's still linger (for that is their fate)
Of the unspeakable horror of May Sixty-Eight
Oh Mary, poor Mary. Oh where did you go?
Do you lurk in dark alleys, in the shadows so bold?
Will Mary-Bell come and "getcha"
If you don't do as you're told?

So ends the story of small Mary Bell,
No innocent girlhood, but a life of pure Hell.
And what moral be gleaned from this short tale
of woe?
Can she give us an answer? What more can
we know?
Came Mary's soft whisper, "You reap what
you sow!"

Pinaforifera

Oh Winifred, you slumber; crowned by marble cross,
Below hard stone
A little plot on High gate hills which rise above
the loam
Kindred spirits we, who rendezvous despite the
forbearing gloam
Once you pranced about the summer heather on
Albury Heath
Then laid rest where mossy-mound gently covers
you beneath
With sightless turn towards Heaven's gate
Surely The Lord your soul did take.
"This Pinaforifera," her Father called:
"The daughter of my tears."
Yet, all these years' lain preterit as winter begets
winters bare.
And whence I espied her chiseled name, she
beckoned me
To linger there.
Her feeble whispers in the wind, of a merry life,
she told.
Of raindrops upon a grassy blade; faerie rings and
balls of gold.

And here stood I so mutable, before the sequent repartee
And knelt beside your tomb Eternal; a reminder of the
Fates that be..
Woe Atropos! Hold close to breast, her diminutive spot,
As near, a night-shade casts its shadow
Upon my fluttered heart!

Albury Heath - Where Winifred played as a child.

Winifred – Winifred Vida Canton (W.V.) 1890-1901, daughter of British writer, William Canton

Highgate hills – Highgate Cemetery. Famous cemetery in London, England.

Pinaforifera - Pet name given by her father, William Canton, in *The Invisible Playmate* "Upon my life I am growing imbecile under the influence of this Pinaforifera"

"Daughter of my tears" "-This *child* might well be called the *daughter of my tears* — yet they have not been bitter ones."

"raindrops on a grassy blade "and "*balls of gold*" from W.V.'s poetry in "*Our Poems*" :" In Memory of W. V.

Atropos - - *oldest of the Three Fates,* It was Atropos who chose the mechanism of death and ended the life of each mortal.

Night-shade - Atropos lends her name to the poisonous plant *Atropa belladonna* or Deadly Nightshade and to the alkaloid atropine

Early and Misc. Poems

Cherry Hellos

Sundays after the flowering sun-dance
and my child's wishes into the night
- cherry hellos
my child dressed in her blue
adventures asleep she slowly mouths the time
In a building across the street
a woman cries into her early morning cup.
Her dream is a lifetime adversary
and she sometimes wishes into the night,
"To my children, a cherry hello"

Sister Moon

You are my evening sentinel
lonely listener to my thoughts
so I sleep
Beneath your frozen stare
a shelter
to bear these twilight hours
and in the still air between each passing
mountain wind
I lay underneath to watch
Your silent venture into the day.

ex post facto

your letter was absent
how it must have grinned!
waiting with undue pleasure.
I sat quietly,
marking off the days,
always leaving my better judgments
for interludes of fantasy
But for all its apparent ecstasy
-their playful somersaults
within a pleasant smile,
was each second beginning
its small measure of the hour.

I had a dream last summer
that you would go away
where not even I could find you
and I kept on searching and calling your name.
There was no answer
So, I wished a foolish wish
that I could be you and enter your world
always to have you with me.....
I am now in that pleasant land
Where I am you
afraid to go, or return
slipping into limbo
as outside,
you watch me fade away
where not even you can find me.

Harris Stevens

At the North Pole

He left one day to buy a thing
and found himself lost
between the seasons
wishing everyone a good time.
"I laugh because I am a little crazy!"
"But I am civilized" -he thought
while making his own meat sandwich.
..as one snowflake falls
and above the hills
Lies the Sun,
a laboring mint green fig.

April Smile

Beyond Sunday's bedroom
Tricks then virginal
was my portrait that barely hung
in your smile.
-other moments and
when days felt sharp
slicing the laughter
into shattered screams
behind that hall of loonies
or, if the orchestra
performs again
will they draw from a bassoon note
a sketch of a girl
stretched by my archaic recital?
-but for her,
that wretched burden of maternity
is another April smile returning to the artist.

In the daylight the calm sweeps into the serene
We are beggars that surround the night's lurking
darkness
by talking into mirrors
but must our thoughts linger in the brightness?
In the morning I find you eating your cake of
layered monstrosities
but the weight is light and the colors festive and
merry
Beyond the day there is a certain fog
but true to nature, it lifts
as a sunken heart must when stirred to vibrant
causes.
and when the brooding anarchy passes,
into upturned glasses we must pause to play the game
with a shuffled deck of cards
and be shadows posed one moment in the
daylight.

Two Friends

Walking down cold streets
handing out nickels on a string
Speaking quietly, words of the idyllic
Passing a monstrosity of humanity
pathetic in the knowledge of past happenings
Now, heads down, expelling white vapor
Warming the evening with their lives.

It is raining as I pass your building silently on my
way home.
After so many years
it is sad to have lost your special meaning,
and the drops are clinging to its graying brick
in tearful emptiness.
It can now just gather this one last emotion.
People and fire hydrants mingle together
on each city block alike, and endless.
Their hopes shattered like the stained glass heroes
that have fallen from a demolished church
and I had hoped to prance upon the water
Blue with dancing feet
The moment, silvered with dusk
and the air still heavy on the earth.
I cry low, behind trees
deaf to the tunes of new music smiling.

Michigan Snowflakes 1969

I stopped at the parking lot
to pick up the quarter I left in the pay phone.
The rent was frozen at one dollar a minute
and diesel fuel glued to the pavement
lay waiting for Spring.
I brought heavy duty shocks
and your voice still in California with it's reedy
scream.
Blended and whipped into agitated breaths
by the pounding surf
The Reader's Digest rested on the kitchen table.
Old America with its poster-book facade!
I laughingly look to the North.

Somerset Maugham lived at night
Picasso lived by day.
Complementary nomenclatures
all competing for my time and special review.
The East Coast nerve center of the world
is coursing through my veins like a California
freeway
I have become a sculpture in the basement of a
museum.
It's purpose lost in the dark.

Surf Music

You returned from the bath:
and scented from the evening
Imagine….
Sun tan oils and oceans
on your happy face,
salty arms.
Your matted hair, gleaming like polyethylene cones.
I remember the searing quality of your eyes
which said,
I am not quite a child any longer.
And your breaths were music smiling at the rains
but when you lay still beside me
that warmth was only wishes
In the magic of the day I've often wondered,
who your mother was!

Harris Stevens

Irene of the Destinies

Symphony of the summer hill mourn
lavender meadow's mystic sunrise
willows singing -eternal wind
artful follies of an ancient spring
-cherubs carnation
laughing monmarths and fingered Kate
-languid
sultry sinews forte
beneath -waterfalls-grasp
the carousel where Unicorn flock
rhodium essence for-never ending
those plastic lip-skinned troubadours of the night
visioned voices of the coming Choir
fertile togetherness,
Two is All / One is Never
Twas...a polymorphic Hobby horse

1) Meditations on a Hobby Horse- E.H. Grombach- *"Art and Illusion"*

Virgin Spectator

a marble floating on a crowded lake
Cry of the lily-white
vestige of a horse's mane
Thunder!
Somber dreams-awakened
to a flower woman's maidenhead
while azure lovers walk the wave
free smiles in a looking-glass
sand-less sea-watchers breathe the tide
Erect sword in scabbard
penetrating a timeless ecstasy
Lilacs of a blonde
surrender to its waiting players
blue messengers of the night seek out their
virtuous prey
the triangular mysterious parting rain splash

Harris Stevens

Tiddlers in a Jam Jar

Powder girl of the shady blonde
inhabitant of the Nova clouds;
where erst it shamed
opaque in waxen symmetry
these cheeks where the seed never dies
positioned spot in soft entrance
In the sepulcher-there by the Sea
passive ripple of the demonic scepter
an Eden of bland response
defying the flowing assault
-esoteric wing
planted in subtle commune
Escape with blossomed fantasies sealed
purged by, which remained purloined jasmine
Tender fair haired lace
like the lone Albatross in a world of moan.

Misanthrope

an unfinished scream
from which I wake up dreaming
of the philosophies which teach nothing
but nihilistic memories
The phobia of an adolescent sonnet
again she became something of a conglomerate
every bit of wisdom used only to ponder
her own memories.
Take the day before June
for instance:
each dumb mountainous thing
munches on this week's favorites
while Violet adjusts
a simian brain-wave modulator
on her kid.
She never stopped with this hair teasing thing
but she had to lose her child in the crowd.
He is sitting behind her in the bus
eating from the Book of Knowledge
he is on page two
and knows enough...
Time marches on
and he may as well be standing
on his head for all the good it does.

The Next President's Hat

(a fable)

I once knew a girl who named her dog, "The Next President's Hat"
Nobody could say why she did this?
Her mother believed the daughter to be gifted, and so...
had her tested by a psychologist who was not very impressed
even though she could name all the presidents.
Thinking she must be psychic, her father
(who had been to Woodstock)
drove her to see an ex-girlfriend who lived on a houseboat,
reading Tarot cards and palms.
The woman wanted to find out who would be the next Chief of State
as she had always been keenly attuned to spectral vibrations
and sensed that the Key to the mystery would reveal itself in the chromatic.

The child was asked, "What color is the next president's hat?"

"White, with brown spots all over!" the little girl
replied.

The seer, believing this to be a portent of "Evil"
rushed the pair quickly out the door, as Exorcism was
not her style.

When the girl was a bit older, she took the dog to
the park.

One day, a man started following her, and when she
sat down on a bench
the stranger approached...

Feigning friendliness, he asked her the dog's name.
She replied, " The next president's hat."

Thinking this kid was too weird, the man
wandered off,
muttering that he might have better luck at the zoo.

The local tabloids got wind of this and made
quite a fuss at the time.

The notoriety bequeathed mixed blessings,
for at school, her teachers could not help but raise
their eyebrows,
trying not to stare, but at least her friends
thought it was cool.

When she turned 18, the dog died, and with collegiate
pursuits she distanced herself from the
imaginations of childhood.

Finally, career, and homemaking became her only
passions.

She decided when he was six, to buy a dog for
her son,
persuading him that the only appropriate name
for the pet was Ralph!
The boy didn't mind this at all, but found himself
secretly calling the dog...."Wittgenstein!"

1) The meaning of a word is its use in the context of language-
   Wittgenstein
2) "When I use a word, it means what I choose it to mean, neither more
   nor less. "Humpty Dumpy-Lewis Carroll- *Through the Looking Glass.*

Yes Virginia, there is an Albatross!

My flight takes the form of Wings
My Songs fly on tracks
Though an evil man may split
His barley soup in half
He will not offer you this little bit of Truth...
Steam engines are as graceful as
evaporating thoughts.

A soft reminder is waiting-
This winter has come and gone
And though there will be others
You will build your castle of the dawn
Each room houses dreams of fortune
closets contain your pain
Its gardens grow new beginnings
As you walk down the flowered paths
Hand in hand with smiling fingers
The avengers gone at last.
Through its corridors and mazes
You meet messengers of Before
But East you will greet a fantasy
And though wingless, you will soar.
Into a Grand contentment
The purveyor of Mystic things
While in the sun room
I find you sleeping Among the dawning of your
Dreams.

The Freudian Horror Show

Do you enjoy the digging into your Mind
Behind closed doors?
All day we bury the Truth
Night time is for unearthing dead pasts
In HIS book of notes your thoughts are naked.

Unspeakable words go unsaid
As many a true thought.
I sleep away the world
for no one can kill a dying man.
Can I love You?
Robber of the Innocent- am I one?
Your face-so puzzled, tinged with unknown fear.
Your eyes overflowing to the brink of tears
Which only made me feel closer.
How heartless it is to love someone you wish to be
...knowing the child will end.

Recent Poems, Essays, and Poems for Sophie

Harris Stevens

HATSUKOI

(Japanese: first bittersweet love)

The clarions of spring ring out
A cadence of majestic song
Like a cannonade of fire
First love of youth, its brilliance burns
Until faded essence gone.

Bye and bye the decades pass
Away from that first sweet dew
Remembrance its only bearer, and gray its only hue.
The weight of this first encounter resides in one's
furtive thumping breast,
And like an errant pebble stepped
It is singular from the rest.

Woe to time that enemy, but whose track we
must abide.
Which tinges and diminishes
Those many years apart.

First love, first true love
Where that diminutive stone abides
The mnemonic crystal within my heart.
Its solemn ode solidifies.

Hatsukoi, Hatsukoi.
Oh how bittersweet...
Like gossamer wind blown Sakura blossoms
laying carpet beneath one's feet.
Hatsukoi, Hatsukoi,
Its joyful, childish sway
Imperious to Eternity, until one's dying day.

Harris Stevens

The Grey Crow's Island

A poem about Oscar and Isola Wilde

Oh sister sweet, Oh sister dear
My heart grew soft when you were near.
Your countenance to gaze
Must I look high above?
While you rest pious below, devoid of love.
Love so sweet, our love so dear
Pure of sin, but so I fear
Though innocent of wayward touch
God Almighty rebukes as such.
To the warmth, your bed, I silently steal as
you call for the light,
When night shivers cause disquiet and fright.
And I, perfumed by this small brazen sprite,
Immersed under covers embraced and held
tight like the warm glowing hearth on a
midwinter's night.
I remember games in the garden
as we skipped hand in hand.
No sorrows beheld in our childish land.
Playmate true, Light of the Clan

Behold nature's spring tide where your feet
touched the sand.
A scant decade of summers before a cold
winter's storm brought life's dying day.
In the gloom of the churchyard, I knelt where you lay.
Only two summers older, I swore I would stay
Forever and ever, a pact I had made
until strong arms came upon me, from your grave
dragged away.
Why do we kill the ones we love?
Some young, some old, by cruel hand we must,
Do it softly "with riches of gold"
Or the ever sharp knife's edge of lust.
A second sin? My lifetime dirge
But the first! Cut life short, love shattered sweet?
Bright remembrance until in Death we meet.
Now years hence provide some solace from touch,
Though thy spirit remains while your bones turn
to dust.
Nearer and nearer, I hear your faint call,
as I fight with the paper that covers the wall.
Impassioned embrace, I clutch all that
remains, a poor, poor memento of my heart,
How it stains!

In decorate illumination possessed
Feebly as my eyes must now rest
Upon this small token,
All that is left.
My last earthly endeavor, though I cannot forebear
To touch the singular lock of your precious
blonde hair.
So it ends, the vast bitter days,
Isola my love, REQUIESCAT in pace!

Footnotes:
1) "Light of the Clan"-Oscar called Isola "the sunlight, or sunshine of the family.
2) New evidence suggests Wilde considered his homosexual affairs his second sin. implying Isola was the first.
3) "I fight with the paper that covers the wall.."
   Oscar Wilde's last words on his deathbed, droll humor to the end., "The wallpaper and I are having a fight, one of us must go!"
4) The Grey Crow's Island:
   Oscar's college nickname was the "grey crow".
5) Isola means island in Italian.
6) The Italian/Latin/ Ecclesiastic pronunciation of "PACE" is Pa-che.
7) Oscar Wilde carried an illustrated envelope containing a lock of Isola's hair throughout his life.

For Nathalia

(For child poetess and prodigy, Nathalia Crane: *The Bard of Brooklyn*)

The Brook-lined streets, old Soap Suds Row,

The symmetries of eons past,
Your words, in childish meter, set the literary
world aghast.
Some serious, some in jest,
The tale of an aged Mandarin
And the Little Rose of Rest.

From Prospect Park and Flatbush,
Your meanderings around the block,
A seer of portent true,
As provenance, stayed the ticking clock.

Between the concrete spires,
Interspersed with tiny gardens
That held the feted Rose,
You swayed, immersed in childhood's dance,

To be written down, by line and row
The tales of dear Marge and Margaret, and
red-haired Roger I suppose?

Nathalia, your words will linger
Like the scent of honey sweet,
There upon, the ancient goddesses will lay roses at
your feet.
A little girl of letters!

Each turn of page a pinnacle reached
Eclipsing the Mountains of the Moon, and lofty
Belos peak.
When "forever afters" have ceased to be

And the Judgment Day is neigh,
To those whoever drew a breath

Resigned to "once upon a time... "
Your words like token symbols sent,

Might stay Humanity's mournful cry.
For among all Worldly sorrows
Such gladness was supplied,
Even though the Earth be but a speck of dust

In the Universe's eye.

A Lament

Ah to be a girl, all slim and fit
To have no parts that do not fit.
Scent of strawberry, golden hair
Bows and ruffles, without a care.

Whether rough and tumble, or dainty and nice
Oh what joy to have a little girl's life.
But to be grownup, for that is my fate
It's really the thing I most truly hate.

As I silently lay alone in my bed
Dreaming of long golden locks
Surrounding my head,
With little pink bows, to keep them tidy and neat,
The ultimate fancy as I fall to sleep.

It is only then I can be who I am,
And eschew the reality of being a man.

No, I will never have those feminine charms
A dear child swaddled in a mother's arms,
Or to hold onto my daddy's big hand

As he tells me I'm the prettiest girl in all the land.
So fantasy driven, I withdraw from the scene
And envelope myself in a non-fulfilled dream.

Now my poor body is shriveled and old
But still, like a child, I must do as I'm told
Alas, without the magical whimsy forsooth,
Of a little girl's carefree nature, and youth.

Dolls

In a darkened back room, somewhat shut away
There are dolls galore.
Some made by an artist's hand
Some bought in second hand stores.

The dolls all have names, and all have a place
Each one is so dear to me
For in my heart there but resides
What others cannot see.

In old Japan, dolls had souls they believed,
And so this tale was conferred to me.
When a beloved ningyo "died" they reverently bowed
Sending its funeral pyre out to the sea.

Some think they are just toys, and not meant for
boys, quizzically peering into my room

Blind to the art and history there,
Looking at the dolls who stare
Back from the protecting gloom.

Harris Stevens

Dolls are for girls with long locks and curls
That is the way of the world
But a "princess pan" locked up in a man
Is a story that needs to be told.

For what they don't see, but is all true to me,
Dolls are mirrors of wishes deep.
A lifetime apart from my childhood heart,
They are shadows of what I never can be.

1. "Ningyo" 人形 The word for doll in Japanese

A Cacophony of Crickets

She sat on the porch as the day meandered
into summer twilight.
Petrichor still heavy in the wake of a distant
passing storm awoke dreamy, sleeping
memories.
An electric memorial to her once-lived
boyhood years.
Sophie's mind was silent and peaceful,
Only marred by the cacophony of crickets
chirping in her ears.

Harris Stevens

A little boy's Fancy

Could I have been a pretty girl
If invaded by the knife?
Throwing off the mantle worn
Would it have been a better life?

I dared not speak, or dared to think
The unsaid words inside,
So to myself and those who sought,
The truth was but a lie.

Now I sit, watching the Sun
Surrender to the evening sky
And with the latent passing years,
I ask myself, "But why"?

KALI

Inside me is a scream
That if let out, would shatter the Universe.
She was my dog. My grand dog. My perpetual
puppy!
She was old in dog years.
17 and a half years or 6,350 days...
Then again, she was a Chihuahua and they say some
live over 20.
And she WAS such a good girl!
For almost 2 decades I loved, worried, and fretted
about her.
The many happy days of nose-licks and demanding
barks for some of "Grampy's" food, and how she loved
my petting her ruff!
However there were those frantic late night rushes to
the emergency clinic,
and my neurotic incessant calls of "Where's Kali"
reverberating from the backyard, the neighborhood,
or the dog park.
Yes, she was an old dog.
Complete with a list of aliments that we tried to
keep under control.

All the sighs of relief through the years as the
doctors
said she would pull through
But finally she couldn't anymore.
She tried her best, but time was too great an
adversary.
On her last day, as we hysterically drove to the
late night clinic.
We hoped...I hoped she would somehow pull
through again.
I always said that as long as she still ate, and was in
no pain...(how she loved her ice cream) I would do
what ever it took to keep her with us.

But she HAD stopped eating...even her ice
cream, and
she WAS in pain which WOULD not go away.
The doctors said it WAS the right thing ....
She looked quite peaceful laying in her little bed as I
played with her ruff for the last time.

When the doctor gently found a vein I HAD to leave
the room....
I could not watch the transition from "IS" to "WAS"
As the needle went in...her life ebbed out.
…..And she WAS such a good girl.

"Turn on the Cozy Lights!"

Please turn on the cozy lights", the little girl implored! I look back into her child eyes, that are wide with anticipation as they meet mine.. and I wonder, and I question, what is the nature of "coziness"? Is it only Providence within the rhythms of childhood? Can only a child fully enjoy this state of being, and what does it mean anyway?

I know adults claim to occasionally experience it. For example, curled up on the eve of a summer storm, book in hand, a woman propped up on her sofa, knees bent, legs tucked under, a gentle throw about her as the imagery of an author's whim draws her away momentarily from the "realms of the real"

But as I reflect on the sing song refrain of this child who continues on incessantly until I do her bidding, I'm drawn into the world she inhabits, and ruefully, I do not. In her domain, COZY is more....

It is a special wonder that I struggle to remember. It is much more than the thrill of an 8 year old's Christmas morning. More so than the annual visit to a theme park or a family road trip. And though those worldly adventures last for many hours or many days, the momentary subtle bliss of "coziness" lives in the infinity of a second. Serene in it's station, it comes and goes quietly like a stalking cat; small as the internals of an atom, and yet unfathomable as the end of time.

Whether it derives from a parent's caress as the child snuggles up against the warm flesh that gave her life, or a singular living memory; a cadence within one's self, realizing both in body and mind that all is right with the world.

An adult analyzes experiences, but the young child "feels". She does not try to understand.

It just IS...

"Cozy" may just be the space between moments, the interval between musical notes the Eastern philosophers call *ma*, which though stagnant, provides a sublime solace.

This is the delicious perfection in which children resonate, and as we have been told, only God is perfect. Is then the meaning of coziness? The world turned inward but beyond self reflection or recognition? The contemplation of a sigh? The blue note in a mystic rhapsody? A timeless silence when we are able to hear the voice of our own soul? Heaven on Earth? A peek into Nirvana? The life long quest sought by Gurus or Zen masters? Or maybe it is the invisible arms of God reaching out in a transitory celestial embrace?

I am not sure, but as the laws of parsimony dictate, I contemplate the forthright simplicity of a child's mind. Whether innocent or naive, the child is both omnipotent, and impotent. Though adults hold dominion over the world, it is won at a severe cost. Few of us will ever rise above the insignificant.

But curled up in her bed, not quite asleep, among daydreams of fairies, unicorns, princes and princesses, the child for a moment IS perfection, and "cozy" is when the world stops to take notice.

Yes, child, I will turn on the cozy lights!

The Wind Chill Factor

There is a chilling that threads the air
And greets me face to face
Which tempers the impassioned heat above
By its cooling, tart embrace.
Effulgent Spring-Tide, its vanguard bowers,
Now dreamily draw to close.
The vestige of a summer's end, gone gentle in
repose.
A precipice slays my triumphant gaze
When Winter's Sun is set upon,
No more to hear the ringing bell
No chime of its device will sound.
And phantasmic glories ne'er partake
As Autumnal leaves of umber crowned.
She sat, behest by *enfant* decree
On her Lupercalic throne!
A Queendom unapproachable
And servitude yet unknown.
Not once, or twice, nor thrice.
A swatch of time's rare garments sewn
Is all that need suffice.
The "One" the simple state of youth
Of "Two" be love entwined,
"Thrice" a tempting of bounties hence

Hope's portal, once resigned.
From the long past's mystic visage,
I heard her Siren's call.
Now ignored and forgotten as a distant foreign
shore,
Only weighty silence fills this everlasting void.
My heart it quivers irregular,
Entranced by boundless energies
Of frivolous Nature, young...
For the Garden's promise of vibrant bloom
Is now the Tomb of "once!"

Harris Stevens

The Girl in the Mirror

The girl smiled at herself in the mirror.
Her reflection smiled back in mutual admiration.
Short straight bangs of fire red.
Skin, vampire white, the color of fresh cream
left by the milkman on the door stoop
yesterday
with no hint or thought of anything but now.

She saw all this with her ice-blue eyes,
and the friendly reflected continence
that she saw standing there gave her the thrill of
being.
Whether clothed in frilly dress or nothing at all,
It was enough.

Looking around her, surrounded in pink,
stuffed animals and dolls strewn about,
she knew that the girl in the mirror would always
be there to comfort her.
Recalling her dream of the night before, she
shuddered,
remembering a nightmare dark and uncanny,
that was almost unfathomable.

In the dream, she stood before the mirror
and what stared back was not the crimson haired
child in bows and ruffles that was herself...
but an old man with saddened eyes, full of regrets.
and long-lost wishes.

Without a thought, the girl reached out, touching
the mirror.
At the same time the man, his face carrying the
weight of so many years followed suit with a
choreographed simultaneous response.

Their fingers almost met but for a few millimeters
of hardened glass
that vanquished all illusion of transparency.

The man's eyes gazed at the girl in the mirror
longingly,
with a stifled sigh pondering what might have been.

The girl stared back defiant, with a duality of
both horror and relief
that on HER side of the mirror she still was...

It had been a puzzling dream for sure,
but soon forgotten
In the brightness of the morning sunlight as she
ran out to play.

Harris Stevens

Little Girl World

little bird dies by reflection
little girl born of deception
are you there
(where)
in the world are you hiding,,
here I am in the closet.
is it safe to come out now?
(it is)
if you open the door quite slowly,,
there's a man outside
(i'm scared)
don't fret dear, but beware
disguise yourself behind my mustache
show off your sparkly nails and Sunflower tresses
combat boots and pussy cat dresses
(it's ok)

2))
wear colors bright
play in the darkness of night.
(what am i)
a boy-girl I suppose
in the middle of a room
(i stand)
A suicide, sniffing a Paper rose"

(with apologies to ee cummings)

A Singular Girl

(For MS)

Sometimes you scare me.
Lightning bolts from your eyes.

Leader of the pack, the Alpha-child.
So why am I not surprised?

Defying the Laws of Clausius.
Transforming Ice into Fire.

One Atom's spark is all you need
To fulfill your heart's desire.

Girl!

Stand proud, while others look askance.
Do not sway or wander.

Animated by the Devil's dance,
or the steadfast hand of God's romance?

You linger, as you are, but for a moment.
A ghost-like memory passing through my mind.

All that ever was, or would be dear,
will age, like fragrant mellow wine.

Time, she cannot be slowed or stopped.

Nor dissuaded from her course.
I do but sometimes conjure hence by will or force.

The continence of your untamed spirit,
that the envious ancient furies stole.

Captured by a creased and faded image yet,

The solitary proof possessed.
A visage of the sweetest soul.

I AM SOPHIE!

Knock, knock, Who's there?
It's me, Sophie
I am…!
I want out..now!
I am Sophie. I am she.
Let me BE!
Away from pain and scorn
I want to be reborn.
Do you see me?
I am Sophie!
I hide..afraid, I linger beneath
The depths of the deep,...deepest soul.
I want out NOW!
Prisoner of memories lost.
I wait inside the boy that never was…
In a womb-like mind I am nurtured, but forever
trapped.
I am SOPHIE! And that's a fact.

www.ingramcontent.com/pod-product-compliance
Lightning Source LLC
Chambersburg PA
CBHW051849040426
42447CB00006B/761